Amish
Cooking
for Kids

Amish Cooking for Kids

FOR 6- TO 12-YEAR-OLD COOKS

Phyllis Pellman Good
Kate Good
Rebecca Good

Illustrations by Cheryl Benner

Good Books

Intercourse, PA 17534
800/762-7171
www.GoodBks.com

Illustrations by Cheryl Benner
Design by Dawn J. Ranck

AMISH COOKING FOR KIDS
Copyright © 1995, 1999 by Good Books, Intercourse, PA 17534
First published in 1995. (ISBN: 1-56148-131-9)
REVISED EDITION, 1999.
International Standard Book Number: 978-1-56148-249-8; 1-56148-249-8
Library of Congress Catalog Card Number: 94-40586

Library of Congress Cataloging-in-Publication Data
Good, Phyllis Pellman
    Amish cooking for kids : for 6- to 12-year-old cooks / Phyllis Pellman Good, Kate
Good, and Rebecca Good.
       p. cm.
    Includes index.
    1. Cookery, Amish--Juvenile literature. 2. Amish--Social life and customs--Juvenile
literature. I. Good, Kate. II. Good, Rebecca.
III. Title
TX715.G61723   1994
641.5'66--dc20   94-40586
                                          CIP
                                          AC

Table of Contents

Introduction

WHO ARE THE AMISH AND WHAT DO THEY EAT?

The Amish are some of the best cooks in North America!

The Amish are a group of people who believe it is important to take good care of their families and good care of the land. They work hard—many of them are farmers—and so they like to eat good food and enjoy it! Their religious faith holds them together and helps them live differently from the rest of the world.

LIVING WITHOUT CARS AND ELECTRICITY

The Amish choose to live simply. They know how easy it is to get so busy that you are away from home a lot and don't have time to be together. And so they drive horses and buggies instead of cars, because then it's harder to run around as much. They live without electricity, which means everyone has to help work together—and there's no arguing about who will watch TV when and how much, because there is no TV. Or radio.

WEARING HOME-SEWN CLOTHES

Amish mothers make most of their family's clothes. All the women and girls in the church community wear similar clothing. All men and boys dress nearly alike. The clothing is simple and easy to live in, and it is much like their grandparents and great-grandparents wore.

This all means that their clothing doesn't go out of style. And Amish people aren't as likely to be jealous of their friends' clothes, because they all have almost the same dresses and aprons or shirts and broadfalls (the kind of pants the men and boys wear).

WORKING TOGETHER

Most Amish families have a big garden. Most Amish families have a stay-at-home mom. Most Amish families have their grandparents or aunts and uncles and cousins living nearby.

When it's mealtime, the food usually comes from the garden—it's either fresh, frozen, or canned. And there is often more than one cook in the kitchen. Mom (or "Mamm," as Amish children say) is almost always there, along with several helpers. When you work together, the job doesn't seem as long or as hard. You can sing and tell stories and teach each other shortcuts. And all the while you're learning how to cook.

That is the way Amish children learn to make the tasty dishes that have been favorites of their families for a long time.

EATING OLD FAVORITES

The Amish like to eat big feasts whenever they get together—to work or to visit or to celebrate. The special foods they serve are like the ones their grandparents (and their many great-great- great-grandparents) ate before them.

The Amish also like to learn from other people. When they see their neighbors eating something that looks and smells really good, they ask for the recipe. Or if they spot a tasty recipe in a store-bought cookbook or on a food package, they like to try it (if they have the ingredients in their garden or pantry).

So their dinner tables and lunch pails sometimes have a mix of old and new foods.

Amish kitchens don't have microwaves or blenders or mixers or food processors (remember—no electricity!). We explain how to make some recipes using these appliances because most homes have them. The food will still taste the same as when an Amish cook makes it.

EATING FROM THE GARDEN

Amish cooks sometimes go to the grocery store. But more often they run out to the garden or down to the basement or over to their neighbor's freezer to gather the ingredients they need. (Many families rent freezer space from their neighbors who have electricity.) A store truck makes weekly visits to some Amish homes, bringing the supplies that Amish families can't grow themselves.

Even if you have to go to the grocery store to buy almost everything you need to cook, try to choose as many fresh foods as you can that are grown near your home area. Then you'll come close to the wonderfully bright flavor of Amish cooking!

LOOK FOR THE QUILT PATCHES

Look at the beginning of each recipe for a drawing of a quilt patch. If you see one patch, you are looking at a recipe that is easy to prepare. If you see four patches, you are looking at a recipe that is more difficult. Then you should ask an adult to help you, unless you've had a lot of experience cooking. Recipes with two or three patches are a medium level. Read them before you begin, to see if you need help.

May you enjoy both making—and eating—this food!

Easy

Medium

Medium

Hard

5

A Few Things You Should Know About Cooking

(especially before you begin!)

1. Always read the recipe the whole way through to the end before you begin to cook.

2. Do you have all the ingredients you need?

3. Do you have enough time to make the recipe?

4. Always check with your grown-up helper about the recipe you want to make. Does she or he agree with your idea?

5. Always be sure that your grown-up helper is available and willing to be with you when you want to cook. Do not cook when you are alone.

6. Be sure to wash your hands before you begin.

7. It's a good idea to wear an apron if you have one.

8. Choose clothing without baggy sleeves or loose tops that could catch on appliances or swoosh through the food.

9. Before you begin, tie back your hair if it's long.

10. Ask for help if you don't understand something.

11. Ask for help if a container is too heavy or hot to handle yourself.

12. Ask your grown-up helper to help you put food into and take food out of the oven.

13. Turn the handles of pans to the back of the stove so you don't bump into them and knock the pans down.

14. Remember, an electric stove stays hot for awhile after it is turned off.

15. Watch out for the open flame on a gas stove that is turned on.

16. Be sure that any container you put in the microwave is microwave-safe.

17. Be sure your hands are dry before you turn on any appliance.

18. Unplug the mixer and blender when you are done using them so they don't switch on accidentally when you are taking them apart to clean them.

19. Be sure you know which side of a knife blade is the sharp side. Always cut and chop with that side away from you.

20. Handle graters and peelers carefully—they may not appear to be as sharp as they are.

21. It is a good idea to put an ingredient back in its place when you're finished using it. It is also a good idea to clean up the splashes and puddles as you go along!

22. When you are finished cooking—and before you sample what you've made—put away any ingredients that are still sitting around. Then gather together all the dirty dishes and utensils, wipe the counter and work area, and help clean up the mess!

A Word to Grown-Up Helpers

1.   Be willing to yield your space to the child who is cooking. While a child should never be left alone to cook, be prepared to let the child occupy your kitchen as fully as necessary.

2.   Try as much as possible to serve as an advisor and coach, rather than being in charge.

3.   Patience will be required of you! Remember that efficiency is not the highest value in this experience.

4.   Practice flexibility! You'll need it. Kids like to experiment with new ingredients and different procedures than given. They may get tired of the process part way through.

     You might want to give some guidance in choosing a recipe since some are more involved, demanding, and time-consuming than others.

     Through it all, remember to be an encourager!

5.   Realize and accept the fact that children enjoy the tactile experience of cooking—the way a batter feels as it changes from runny to stiff; the life in bread dough when kneading it; the tearing of lettuce leaves; chopping of fruit chunks; watching broth boil; smelling a pie baking.

     Children are as interested in the process of cooking as they are in the final product.

6.   Expect messes! Show the child how to clean them up, cheerfully.

7.   While most Old Order Amish do not have microwaves, blenders, mixers, and other electrically powered appliances in their homes, many of these recipes suggest their use. That is because we believe children should learn to use the appliances that they have in their own kitchens. Furthermore, those changes in method do not affect the flavor of the final result.

8.   Use the occasion to learn about the Amish, an unusual people who value children, good food, and the land from which it comes.

     The recipes, supporting text, and illustrations can open this world as you cook together with a child. Here is an indirect way to teach respect for others who are different.

9.   Consider taking the child along grocery shopping. That will enlarge the child's understanding of the whole food process.

10. Cooking puts kids in touch with elemental food that is not prepackaged or served at a drive-in window or by a waiter.

     Cooking is a natural activity for kids. And it is a valued child-adult activity.

     Allow your own sense of discovery and wonder to be renewed—along with the child's!

BREAKFAST

It is early morning and the gas lights still hiss in the kitchen when the family comes in from doing the chores in the barn. Mamm got up early to cook a breakfast of eggs, scrapple, and cornmeal mush. Homemade bread and jelly, applesauce, and shoofly cake are already on the table.

The family gathers around the table with Datt at the head. They all bow their heads and pray silently. Datt's loud sigh signals that the prayer is over. Everyone picks up a serving dish.

The family begins to eat.

BREAKFAST MENU

* Eggs, Sunny-Side Up
  Scrapple or Cornmeal Mush
* Applesauce or Home-Canned Fruit
  Stewed Crackers or Pancakes
* Shoofly Cake

* recipes are in this book

Sunny-Side Up Eggs

Makes 2 servings

INGREDIENTS

- 1$\frac{1}{2}$ Tbsp. butter or margarine, or non-stick cooking spray
- 2 eggs
- water
- salt (optional)

EQUIPMENT

- Frying pan or skillet (medium-sized)
- Small bowl
- Cup
- Metal spatula
- Plastic spatula

1. Put chunks of butter or margarine in the frying pan. Turn the burner on to low heat. Let the butter or margarine melt. Tilt the pan so that the butter or margarine runs all over the bottom of it.

If you are using spray instead, spray the inside of the pan. Make sure that the whole bottom of the pan is covered.

5. When the white part of the eggs turns from clear to white, the eggs are cooked. To test if they are cooked the whole way through, slide a metal spatula carefully underneath the eggs. If the egg whites are still runny, the eggs are not finished. Keep testing them until they are set and fully cooked. It usually takes 1-2 minutes after they are put in the hot pan to cook.

6. When the eggs are finished, slide the metal spatula underneath one egg and lift it onto the plate. Do the same thing for the second egg.

7. To add a little flavor to the eggs, sprinkle them with salt.

2. Crack an egg on the edge of a small bowl until there is an opening in the shell. Do not crack too hard or the whole shell will break.

When you have cracked the shell, hold onto both ends and pull them apart. Let the egg drop in the small bowl. Do it carefully so that the yolk does not break.

Throw the shell away. If a piece of the shell falls into the bowl, get it out with a fork, being careful not to break the yolk. Do the same thing with the second egg.

3. Fill a cup half full of water. Dip your fingers in it, then spray some water into the frying pan. If it sizzles, the pan is hot enough to cook the eggs.

4. Carefully pour the eggs into the frying pan. Try not to break the yolks. Use a plastic spatula to clean the bowl after you have poured the eggs into the pan.

Applesauce

Makes 6-8, ½-cup servings

Skill Level: ◆ ◆ ◆

INGREDIENTS

- 2-2½ pounds of apples
  (5 or 6 medium-sized ones)
- 1½ cups water
- ½-¾ cup sugar

EQUIPMENT

- Paring knife
- Cutting board
- 3- or 4-quart saucepan
- Measuring cups
- Wooden spoon
- Food press
- Large baking pan or dish pan
- Plastic spatula

1. Scrub the apples well. Lay them, one by one, on the cutting board and cut them in half.

2. Ask your adult helper to cut out the apples' cores and any spots you see. (The apples do not need to be peeled.)

3. Lay the apple halves on the cutting board and cut the halves in half. Then put all the pieces in the saucepan.

4. Measure in the water and cover the pan. Set it on the stove.

5. Turn it on to a medium heat. Stir the apples up from the bottom every 5 minutes. That will keep them from sticking. It will also help them to cook evenly. They will need about 30 minutes to cook until they're soft.

6. Stand the food press in a large pan.

7. When all the apples are mushy, spoon them carefully into the food press in the large pan. Remember the apples are hot and a little splash can burn!

8. Press the apples through the press until all that is left inside the sieve are the peelings.

9. Clean the legs and outside of the press with the plastic spatula, and take them out of the pan.

10. While the sauce is still hot, stir in $1/2$ cup sugar. When you have mixed it in well, taste a spoonful of the sauce. (Don't burn your tongue!) If you like the flavor, do not add anymore sugar.

If the sauce is a little sour, add some more sugar, up to $3/4$ cup total.

Different kinds of apples have different amounts of natural sugar within them. Some make naturally sweeter sauce than others. That is why you taste-test the applesauce to know how much sugar you need to add.

11. Let the applesauce cool and then eat it whenever you like—for breakfast or a snack, lunch or supper!

Shoofly Cake

Makes 9-12 servings

Skill Level: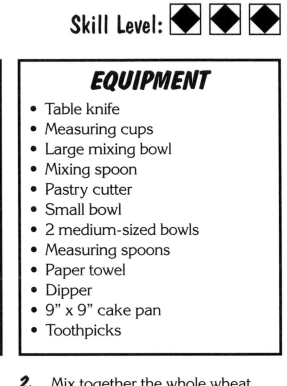

INGREDIENTS

- 1 cup whole wheat flour
- 1 cup white flour
- 1 cup brown sugar
- $1/2$ cup (4 tbsp.) margarine, softened
- 1 cup water
- 1 cup molasses
- 1 tsp. baking soda
- shortening for greasing the baking pan
- flour for dusting the baking pan

EQUIPMENT

- Table knife
- Measuring cups
- Large mixing bowl
- Mixing spoon
- Pastry cutter
- Small bowl
- 2 medium-sized bowls
- Measuring spoons
- Paper towel
- Dipper
- 9" x 9" cake pan
- Toothpicks

1. Get the margarine out of the refrigerator about an hour before you're ready to begin baking. Set it on the counter so it can reach room temperature. Then it is easier to work with when you need it. (If you forget to do this, or don't have time, cut the margarine into $1/2$-inch thick chunks and put them in a microwave-safe small bowl. Microwave on high for 20 seconds, or just until the margarine softens, but doesn't melt.) Set it aside until you need it.

2. Mix together the whole wheat flour, white flour, and brown sugar in a large mixing bowl with a mixing spoon.

3. Put the margarine in with the dry ingredients. Using either your fingers or a pastry cutter, work the margarine into the dry ingredients until the mixture becomes fine crumbs, like little peas.

4. Spoon out $1^{1}/2$ cups of these crumbs into a small bowl and set them aside.

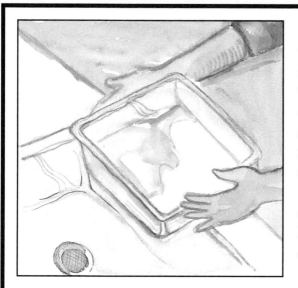

10. Put a heaping Tbsp. of flour into the greased pan. Hold the pan, tilting it slightly, with one hand. Bump the pan with your other hand so the flour lightly dusts the pan's whole bottom and sides. Keep turning the pan so the flour falls onto each part of the inside surface.

Do all this over the sink so you don't have clouds of flour on the floor! Dump any extra flour that didn't stick onto the sink or a waste can.

5. Pour 1 cup of water into a microwave-safe bowl that holds 2 cups or more. Cover. Microwave on high for 3 minutes or until the water boils.

6. In a medium-sized mixing bowl combine the boiling water, molasses, and baking soda.

7. Pour the liquid into the large bowl of crumbs. Stir it all together until the batter is thin, but still lumpy.

8. Set the oven to 350°.

9. Using a paper towel dipped in shortening, lightly grease the bottom and sides of the cake pan. (You may spray the inside of the pan with no-stick cooking spray instead.)

11. Using a dipper, spoon the batter into the cake pan. Sprinkle over top the crumbs you set aside earlier.

12. Place the pan on a rack in the middle of the oven. Bake 35 minutes.

13. Test the cake to see if it is done by sticking a toothpick in the middle of the cake. If the pick comes out clean, the cake is finished baking. If the batter or crumbs stick to the pick, put the cake back in the oven and bake it for another 3 minutes.

Continue doing this until the pick comes out clean.

14. Cut the cake into squares and serve warm or cooled to room temperature.

LUNCH PAIL MEALS

Amish schools don't have cafeterias. So everybody brings a packed lunch from home.

Sometimes in the wintertime, when it's so cold that the teacher has to build a fire in the wood or coal stove to heat the building, students (the Amish call them "scholars") warm their lunches on top of this furnace.

Some bring potatoes wrapped in aluminum foil. They lay them on a ledge inside the furnace door so the potatoes are baked by lunchtime.

Some bring soup or pizza or last night's leftovers to warm on top of the heating stove. Imagine how good it smells in the classroom as lunchtime nears!

On other days, lunch is cold sandwiches, along with homebaked munchies from the pantry, and fruit from the orchard or canning shelves.

A LUNCH BOX MENU

* Homemade Bread Sandwich
    with sweet bologna, cheese,
    lettuce, tomato, and mayonnaise
  Celery with Peanut Butter
  Red Beet Egg
  A Peach or Apple or Pear from the
    orchard
* Whoopie Pie
  A Cold Drink —Milk or * Lemonade
    or Meadow Tea

* recipes are in this book

Homemade Bread

Makes 2 loaves

Skill Level: ◆ ◆ ◆ ◆

INGREDIENTS

- $^1/_2$ cup lukewarm water
- 1 package yeast
- 1 tsp. sugar
- 2 cups lukewarm water
- $1^1/_4$ tsp salt
- $^1/_3$ cup sugar
- $1^3/_4$ Tbsp. shortening
- 7-8 cups flour
- shortening
- butter or margarine

EQUIPMENT

- Measuring cups
- Large mixing bowl
- Wooden spoon
- Measuring spoons
- Table knife
- Rubber spatula
- Paper towel
- Tea towel
- Two bread pans
- Fork

1. How do you get lukewarm water? You run water from a sink faucet over your wrist. As soon as the water feels warm, fill a $^1/_2$ cup measure with it and pour it into a very large mixing bowl. (You need a bowl that is big enough that the mixture won't slosh over the sides.) Remember, if the water is too hot, it will kill the yeast and then the bread cannot rise.

You may also use a microwave temperature probe to heat the water to 115°.

2. Cut the yeast package open with a pair of scissors and pour the yeast into the warm water. Stir gently until you don't see the yeast anymore.

3. Pour 1 tsp. of sugar into the bowl. As you pour, stir so that the sugar disappears and you no longer hear it crunching on the bottom of the bowl.

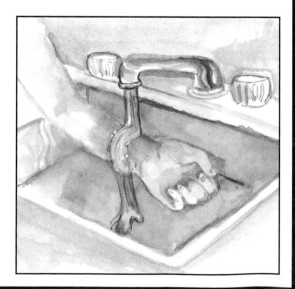

4. Next, stir in 2 cups of lukewarm water (remember how to test that), salt, $^{1}/_{3}$ cup sugar, and shortening. Use a sturdy knife to dig the shortening out of its container and move it into the measuring spoon.

5. Measure 1 cup of flour and add it to the mixture in the bowl. Stir it in so there are no lumps. Keep adding the flour, 1 cup at a time, stirring until the mixture gets very stiff and hard to stir. This should happen after you have added about 6 or $6^{1}/_{2}$ cups of the remaining flour. With a rubber spatula scrape the bread dough off the sides of the mixing bowl.

6. Sprinkle flour lightly over the counter or table where you are going to work with the dough. Also, sprinkle flour lightly over your hands. Now it is time to knead.

7. To knead, push the heels of your hands into the dough. Then turn the dough so that the part you just kneaded is on your right. Fold the top of the dough toward yourself and push the heels of your hands into it again. Keep turning, folding, and pushing until the dough is no longer sticky but is stiff and feels stretchy, like a rubber band. It takes about 8 minutes for it to get this way.

8. Wash the large mixing bowl that you used earlier. After it is clean, take a paper towel and wipe the whole inside of the bowl with a little shortening.

9. Place the dough in the bowl and cover it with a clean towel. Let it rise for about 2 hours in a warm place (an oven with only its light turned on is a good spot). When the dough is about twice its original size, punch it down to its original size.

12. Set the oven to 375°. Put both pans into the oven and bake the bread for 25-30 minutes. Take them out when the tops of the loaves begin to get brown.

13. Carefully, with potholders so you do not burn your hands, put the pans on a wire rack on the counter so they can cool for 10 minutes. (Set a timer to keep track of the time.)

10. Grease two bread pans with a paper towel and some shortening. With your hands, separate the dough into two equal-sized balls and put one in each bread pan. Use a fork to make about 9 to 12 small holes in the top of each loaf.

14. After the 10 minutes are up, use a table knife to carefully loosen the sides of the bread from the pans. When you have done that, turn each pan on its side and shake it gently so the bread comes out. Be careful that it does not fall on the floor!

11. Cover the dough and let it rise until it is higher than the bread pans (about two hours).

15. Rub about 1 tsp. of butter or margarine on the top of each loaf. Then let them cool completely.

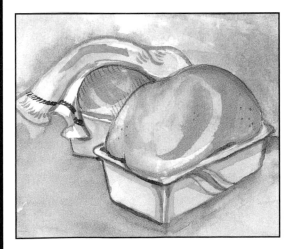

Whoopie Pies

Makes 1 dozen cookie sandwiches   **Skill Level:** ◆ ◆ ◆

Have you ever packed a piece of cake in your lunch, only to find that the icing stuck to the wrapping? Whoopie Pies are a solution to that problem—a cookie sandwich with the icing in the middle!

INGREDIENTS

- $1/2$ cup sugar
- $1/4$ cup shortening
- 1 small egg
- 1 cup flour
- $1/4$ cup baking cocoa
- $1/4$ tsp. salt
- $1/4$ cup milk
- $3/4$ tsp. lemon juice
- $1/2$ tsp. vanilla
- $1/2$ tsp. baking soda
- $1/4$ cup hot water
- shortening or no-stick cooking spray

EQUIPMENT

- Large mixing bowl
- Wooden spoon for stirring
- Electric mixer
- Plastic spatula
- Flour sifter
- Medium-sized mixing bowl
- Two small mixing bowls
- Measuring cups
- Measuring spoons
- Two cookie sheets
- Oven mitts
- Eggbeater
- Table knife
- Paper towel

1. Put $1/2$ cup sugar and $1/4$ cup shortening into the large mixing bowl. Place the bowl under the beaters of the electric mixer. Turn the mixer on to medium speed. Beat ingredients together for 1 minute. Scrape down the sides of the bowl with a plastic spatula.

2. Add an egg and beat again on medium speed for $1/2$ minute.

3. Place the flour sifter in the medium-sized bowl. Measure in the flour, cocoa, and salt. Sift. Let it sit until you need it.

4. Pour milk into the small bowl. Stir in the lemon juice. Set it aside until you need it.

5. Add half the flour mixture to the creamed sugar-shortening-egg mixture. Turn the mixer to a low speed and beat the ingredients for $1/2$ minute. Turn the mixer off. With the plastic spatula, push the batter from the sides down into the bowl.

6. Pour in half the milk/lemon juice. Turn the mixer on again to low and beat the mixture until it is smooth. Turn off the mixer and scrape the sides of the bowl again.

7. Add the rest of the flour mixture. Turn the mixer on again to low and beat until the batter is smooth. Turn the mixer off and scrape the sides of the bowl.

10. Mix at medium speed until the mixture is smooth. Scrape the batter off the beaters and the sides of the bowl.

11. Turn the oven on to 400°. Grease the cookie sheets with shortening or no-stick cooking spray.

8. Add the rest of the milk and lemon juice. When it is mixed in well, add the vanilla. When that is thoroughly mixed in, turn off the mixer and scrape the sides of the bowl.

9. Put the hot water into the other small mixing bowl. Stir in the baking soda (watch it fizz!) and keep stirring until it disappears. Pour that mixture into the batter and turn the mixer on one last time.

12. Drop rounded teaspoons of batter onto the cookie sheet. Keep about 2 inches between the cookies—and between the sides of the cookie sheet and the cookies along the edges. When the cookie sheet is full, slide it into the oven.

13. Bake the cookies for 8-10 minutes, or until they are a little browned around the edges, but still soft. (Fill your second cookie sheet while the first sheet of cookies is baking.) Let them cool about 3 minutes before you lift them off the sheet.

Whoopie Pie Filling

INGREDIENTS

- 1 egg white
- 1 Tbsp. milk
- 1/2 tsp. vanilla
- 1/2 cup confectioners' sugar
- 1/4 cup plus 2 Tbsp. shortening
- 1/2 cup confectioners' sugar

EQUIPMENT

- Small bowl for mixer
- Electric mixer
- Measuring spoons
- Measuring cups
- Plastic spatula
- Table knife

1. Ask a grown-up to help you separate the egg white from the egg yolk. Drop the white into the small bowl for the electric mixer and beat it on medium speed until it is foamy and light.

2. Add the milk, vanilla, and 1/2 cup confectioners' sugar. Mix together on low speed.

3. Add the shortening and beat until fluffy.

4. Scrape down the sides of the bowl and add the other 1/2 cup confectioners' sugar. Scrape the sides of the bowl and the beaters.

5. With a table knife, spread a dab of the filling on the flat side of a cooled cookie (see page 24). Top with another cookie to form a "sandwich" Whoopie Pie!

Lemonade

Makes 8 ½-cup servings

Skill Level:

INGREDIENTS

- 2 lemons
- 1^1/$_2$ cups sugar
- 2 cups hot water
- 1^1/$_2$ quarts cold water

EQUIPMENT

- Cutting board
- Paring knife
- Large mixing bowl
- Microwave-safe medium-sized bowl
- Measuring cups
- Potato masher
- Wooden spoon
- Quart measure

1. Wash the lemons well.

2. Lay one on the cutting board and slice off its two ends. Then cut the lemon into skinny slices. Pick out the seeds whenever you see one.

3. Slide the slices into the mixing bowl, pushing the juice on the cutting board along with the pieces of lemon. Repeat this with the second lemon.

4. Spread the slices over the bottom of the bowl. Measure the sugar and sprinkle it evenly over the slices.

5. Stomp the sugar and lemon slices together with the potato masher. Push it firmly into the slices and then twist it around so you get all the lemon pulp to mix with the sugar. When the sugar and lemon are well mixed and juicy, give your arm a break and heat the water.

26

You may stop stirring when the sugar has disappeared and no longer makes a gritty noise on the bottom of the bowl as you stir.

8. Add the cold water and stir. When it is well mixed, wash your hands. Then reach into the lemonade and fish out the rinds. Squeeze them hard to keep all the good juice in the lemonade. (You may need to do this in several handfuls.) Fish out any seeds you may have missed, too.

6. Pour 2 cups of water into the microwave-safe bowl. Microwave on High for 5 minutes.

9. Set the drink in the refrigerator to cool, or serve it immediately over ice cubes.

7. Pour the hot water over the lemon-sugar juice in the large mixing bowl. Stir it right away so that the sugar can dissolve in the hot water.

SATURDAY AND SUMMER SUPPERS

In Amish families, almost everyone works at home —Mamm (what Amish children call their mothers) is always there; Datt (what they call their dads) is usually there; the big brothers and sisters who have finished going to school are nearly always around. And they all eat three meals a day at home.

On Saturdays and during the summertime, everyone—including the scholars—is home for lunch. At those times, lunch is the big meal of the day. The Amish call that meal "dinner." There's lots of work to be done during the afternoon, so the food at noon is hearty.

By suppertime, everyone is winding down. Saturday and summer evenings often begin with snack-y suppers.

A SATURDAY SUPPER MENU

Soup—either *Chicken Corn or
   Noodle or Potato or *Tomato

Sandwiches—either Fried Egg or
   Sweet Bologna or Tomato and
   Cheese

Sliced Red and Yellow Tomatoes (when
   they're growing in the garden)
   sprinkled with brown sugar

Dessert—either Crumb Cake or Apple
   Dumplings or *Pudding

*Cold Soup or Bread Soup, made
   with blueberries or strawberries or
   sliced peaches

Fruit mush, made with blueberries or
   raspberries or Concord grapes

* recipes are in this book

Chicken Corn Soup

Serves 12-14, 1-cup servings

Skill Level: ◆

INGREDIENTS

- 5 5-oz. cans cooked chicken, cut up
- 2 16¹/₂-oz. cans whole kernel corn, drained (shoepeg is especially good)
  or
- 1 quart frozen or fresh corn
- 3 13³/₄-oz. cans chicken broth
- 8 ozs. noodles or rivels (see recipe for rivels on page 32)
- 2 hard-boiled eggs (See directions for cooking eggs on page 32)
- Dash of pepper

EQUIPMENT

- Four-quart soup pot
- Can opener
- Wooden spoon
- Paring knife
- Cutting board

1. Lay the uncooked eggs on the counter so they reach the temperature of the kitchen as you cook the soup.

2. Put the chicken and corn into the a 4-quart soup pot. Mix together gently with a wooden spoon.

3. Pour the chicken broth slowly over the chicken and corn, so it doesn't splash. Stir it all together.

4. Set the pan on the stove and turn the burner to medium heat. Cover the pan.

5. Stir every 5 minutes until the broth begins to boil. (You'll know it's boiling when it bubbles the whole way across the soup.)

8. While the soup cooks, hard-boil the eggs (see page 32).

9. Turn off the burner that is cooking the soup after 6 or 7 minutes.

10. Gently stir in the cut-up eggs and pepper.

11. The soup's ready to eat!

6. Drop the noodles by handfuls—or crumble the rivels with your thumb and first two fingers —into the bubbling soup.

7. Stir every 2 minutes, mixing up well from the bottom so nothing sticks.

2. Break the egg over the flour.

3. Mix together with a fork until the mixture is dry and crumbly.

4. Crumble into the boiling soup with your thumb and first two fingers.

HOW TO HARD-BOIL EGGS

1. Begin with eggs that are the same temperature as your kitchen. (If you keep them in the refrigerator, set them out about an hour before you need them. That will keep them from cracking as they cook.)

2. Lay the eggs in a small saucepan. Cover them with cool water from the faucet.

HOW TO MAKE RIVELS

Rivels are little doughballs that make the soup thick (instead of noodles) and are fun to bite into!

$3/4$ cup flour
1 egg

1. Put the flour in a medium-sized bowl.

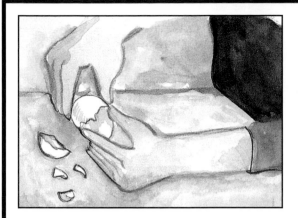

7. Gently peel off the shell. Rinse to get rid of any little pieces.

8. Lay one peeled egg on the cutting board. Cut it in half the long way with a paring knife.

9. Cut each half in two long strips. Cut across each strip, making small squares.

10. Repeat for the second half and the second egg.

3. Place the pan on the stove, uncovered, and turn the burner on high. Heat until the water boils.

4. When bubbles break across the water, take the pan off the stove and set it on a hot pad. Cover the pan.

5. Let it sit 15 to 18 minutes.

6. Pour the eggs and hot water into the sink. Run cold water over the eggs until they are cool enough for you to handle.

Tomato Soup

Serves 6, 1-cup servings

Skill Level:

INGREDIENTS

- 2 cups tomato juice or V-8 juice
- $1/2$ tsp. baking soda
- 1 quart milk
- 1 tsp. salt
- Dash of pepper
- 2 Tbsp. butter or margarine

EQUIPMENT

- 2 saucepans (a one-quart and a two-quart)
  or
- 2 microwave-safe bowls (a one-quart and a two-quart)
- Measuring cups
- Measuring spoons
- Wooden spoon
- Table knife

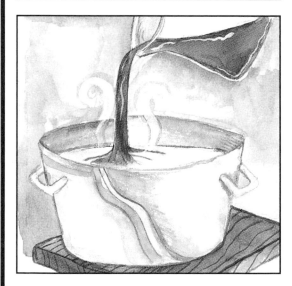

1. Pour the juice into either a one-quart saucepan or microwave-safe bowl. Heat until the juice boils (when little bubbles cover the surface of the juice). It will take about 3 minutes on High in the microwave.

2. When the juice boils, set the pan or bowl on the counter. Stir in the baking soda. Continue stirring until the mixture stops foaming. Set this aside.

3. Pour the milk into the two-quart saucepan or microwave-safe bowl. Heat it until it forms a skin on top but does not boil. This will take about 5-7 minutes on High in the microwave if the milk is cold when you start.

4. Remove it from the stove or microwave and stir in the salt, pepper, and butter. Then carefully pour the hot tomato juice mixture into it.

5. Eat the soup with crackers crumbled into it.

Cold Soup or Bread Soup

Serves 2, ½-cup servings

INGREDIENTS

- 1 slice of bread (homemade tastes best)
- 1 cup fresh fruit
  (sliced strawberries, peaches, bananas, or blueberries)
- 1 cup cold milk

EQUIPMENT

- Soup bowl
- Paring knife
- Cutting board
- Measuring cup

1. Tear up the bread and divide it between two soup bowls.

2. Slice the fruit on the cutting board. Spread the slices over the bread.

3. Measure the milk and pour it over the fruit and bread.

4. Eat it while it's cold —and cool off!

Homemade Vanilla Pudding

Serves 5, ½-cup servings

Skill Level:

INGREDIENTS

- 2 cups milk
- 2 eggs
- 2 Tbsp. cornstarch
- ¼ cup sugar
- ½ tsp. vanilla
- ½ Tbsp. butter or margarine

EQUIPMENT

- 2-quart microwave-safe measure
- Whisk or spoon
- Measuring cups
- Measuring spoons

1. Mix all of the following ingredients together in a 2-quart microwave-safe bowl: 2 cups of milk, 2 eggs, 2 Tbsp. of cornstarch, and ¼ cup of sugar.

2. Mix until smooth, then heat in the microwave, uncovered, on High for 45 seconds.

3. Set the bowl on a hot pad. Stir.

4. Repeat steps 3 and 4 eight times. (Get a piece of paper to keep track of how many times you microwave it.)

5. Then stir in ½ tsp. vanilla and ½ Tbsp. butter.

6. Let it cool for 2 hours. (Eating the pudding before it is fully cooled might upset your stomach.)

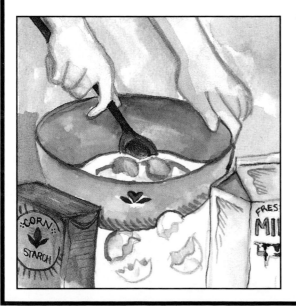

MAIN MEALS

Amish families grow big gardens. They eat some of the peas and beans and corn on the days they pick that food. They can and freeze the rest, so they can eat home-grown vegetables at other times of the year.

Some Amish families butcher a pig and a steer and chickens so they can have meat throughout the year. What they can't eat fresh, they freeze or can or smoke.

The seasons often help Amish cooks know what meals to make.

SPRING

* Homemade Bread with fresh *Strawberry Jam
  New Potatoes with Brown Butter (fresh from the garden)
  Fresh Peas or Sugar Peas (fresh from the garden)
* Salad made with Cutting Lettuce (fresh from the garden)
* Meat Loaf
  Strawberry Shortcake (strawberries fresh from the patch)

SUMMER

* Ham (smoked or frozen) with Green Beans (fresh from the garden) and Potatoes (fresh from the garden)
  Cole Slaw (made with cabbage fresh from the garden)
* Fresh Fruit Salad (fresh from the orchard) with Spice Cake
* Macaronis with Cheese and Hamburger

FALL

* Beef Roast (just butchered) with * Gravy
* Mashed Potatoes (dug from the garden)
* Baked Corn (frozen)
* Pickles
* Applesauce (fresh from the orchard)
* Chocolate Cake with *Caramel Icing

WINTER

* Creamed Dried Beef (smoked, dried beef)
* Candied Sweet Potatoes (dug from the garden)
  or
* Chicken Pot Pie
  Broccoli (fresh from the garden or frozen)
* Vanilla Pudding with Ginger Snaps

* recipes are in this book

Strawberry Jam

Fills about 4 1-cup jars

INGREDIENTS

- 1 quart fresh strawberries
- 2 cups sugar
- 2 cups sugar
- 2 tsp. lemon juice

EQUIPMENT

- Three-quart saucepan
- Cutting board
- Paring knife
- Measuring cups
- Measuring spoons
- Wooden spoon
- Timer
- Jelly jars (one-cup size, if available)

1. Pinch the stems off the tops of the strawberries. Hold each stem tightly, twist it firmly (be careful not to squeeze the strawberry too hard!), and pull up.

2. Lay the strawberries, one at a time, on a cutting board and slice them in halves or in quarters. Put them in the saucepan.

3. Stir in the first two cups of sugar, mixing the berries and sugar together well.

4. Place the saucepan on the stove and turn it on to medium heat. Cook until the fruit boils (when little bubbles dance all over the surface of the jam).

5. The jam should boil gently for 5 minutes. It needs to be stirred with the wooden spoon every minute. You may set the timer for one minute; then stir. Repeat that step 4 more times, making a pencil stroke on a piece of paper each time you do it.

6. Turn off the stove. Set the pan on a hot pad on the counter. Stir in 2 more cups of sugar and the teaspoons of lemon juice. Put the pan back on the stove.

7. Turn the stove on again to a medium heat. Cook the jam once more until it boils. This time it must boil for 10 minutes, and be stirred every minute. Keep track of the time and when you should stir, like you did before.

8. When the jam has boiled for 10 minutes, turn off the stove and set the pan on a hot pad on the counter. Let it sit there for a whole day (24 hours).

9. Spoon the jam into jelly jars. Put yours in the refrigerator until you are ready to use it. Give the other jars to your friends or neighbors or schoolteacher or grandmother.

Salad with Homemade Dressing

Serves 4 or more, 1-cup servings   Skill Level: ◆ ◆

INGREDIENTS

- Lettuce
- Tomato
- Cucumber
- Carrot
- Alfalfa sprouts

DRESSING INGREDIENTS

- 1 Tbsp. honey
- 2 Tbsp. lemon juice
- 1/4 cup oil
- shake of salt
- shake of pepper
- shake of dillweed
- shake of basil

EQUIPMENT

- Big mixing bowl
- Cutting board
- Paring knife
- Vegetable peeler
- Wooden spoon

EQUIPMENT FOR DRESSING

- Glass jar with lid
   (one-pint or one-quart size)
- Measuring spoons
- Measuring cups
- Plastic spatula

1. Wash all the vegetables well.

2. Tear up the lettuce and make a layer of it in the big mixing bowl.

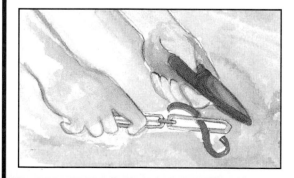

3. Cut out the stem end of the tomato (you may need to ask an adult for help). Set it on the cutting board and cut the tomato in half with the paring knife. Lay the flat side against the cutting board and slice it lengthwise into narrow wedges. Slide the tomato pieces into the mixing bowl.

4. Lay the cucumber on the cutting board and slice off the stem end. Then cut thin round slices until you have as much as you want.

5. Lay the carrot on the cutting board and slice off the stem end. Peel the carrot with the vegetable peeler.

6. When you have gotten rid of the carrot's outer peel, use the vegetable peeler to cut thin, curly slices off the carrot. Keep doing this until the carrot disappears. (Be careful not to slice your fingers as you get near the end. It's better to just eat that last nubby piece!)

Add the carrot slices to the mixing bowl.

7. Put a layer of sprouts in the mixing bowl.

8. Toss the salad ingredients with the wooden spoon or your hands. When the salad is well mixed, set it aside until you have the dressing ready and it's time to eat.

9. Measure all the dressing ingredients into the glass jar. (You'll need the spatula to get all the honey and oil into the jar.)

10. Screw on the lid tightly and shake the jar. Keep shaking until the ingredients look mixed.

11. When it's time to eat, shake the jar again, and then pour the dressing over the salad.

Meat Loaf

Makes 4-6 servings

Skill Level: ◆ ◆

INGREDIENTS FOR MEAT LOAF

- 1 pound hamburger
- $^2/_3$ cup bread crumbs
- $^2/_3$ cup tomato juice
- 1 medium-sized onion
- 1 egg
- $^1/_2$ tsp. salt
- dash of pepper
- shortening

INGREDIENTS FOR GLAZE

- 3 Tbsp. brown sugar
- $^1/_4$ cup ketchup
- 1 tsp. dry mustard

EQUIPMENT

- Large mixing bowl
- Measuring cups
- Paring knife
- Cutting board
- Small bowl
- Fork or whisk
- Measuring spoons
- Strong wooden spoon
- Bread pan
- Paper towel
- Medium-sized bowl
- Plastic spatula

1. Put the hamburger in a large mixing bowl. Measure in the bread crumbs and tomato juice.

2. With a sharp paring knife, carefully cut off both ends of the onion. With your fingers, pull off the papery outer skin of the onion. Lay the onion on a cutting board and cut it in half from top to bottom.

3. Lay the cut side of the onion down on the cutting board. Hold onto the onion with one hand and cut it into skinny lengthwise slices with the paring knife in your other hand.

4. Then cut across the onion crosswise, making skinny slices again. When you finish, you'll have little cubes of onion. Slide them off the cutting board and into the bowl with the hamburger.

5. Crack the egg into a small bowl. Beat it a little bit with a fork or a whisk until the yolk and white are no longer separated. Pour it into the hamburger mixture.

6. Add salt and pepper.

7. Grease a bread pan with a little dab of shortening on a folded-up paper towel. Set it aside until you're ready for it.

8. Mix everything together with a wooden spoon or with your (clean!) hands.

9. When you have mixed the meat evenly, shape it into a big round ball. Then push down gently on the sides so that it becomes a loaf shape.

10. Lift the loaf into the bread pan, pushing the meat to fit the shape of the pan.

11. Turn the oven to 375°.

12. In a medium-sized bowl, stir together the brown sugar, ketchup, and mustard until there are no lumps. Spoon the glaze over the top of the meat loaf, scraping out the bowl with a plastic spatula.

13. Set the meat loaf in the oven and let it bake for one hour.

Fruit Salad

Serves as many as you want, depending on how much fruit you decide to cut up and put together!

Skill Level

INGREDIENTS

• Your favorite fresh fruit, in season—
    apples
    plums
    peaches
    pears
    grapes
    bananas
    blueberries
    apricots
    cantaloupe
    honeydew
    watermelon
    strawberries
    raspberries
    oranges
    grapefruit
    cherries

• Your favorite canned fruit, because it has juice and adds variety—
    peaches
    pears
    apricots
    pineapples
    cherries

EQUIPMENT

• Big mixing bowl
• Cutting board
• Paring knife
• Long-handled spoon for mixing

1.   This dish can be made with your favorite fruits. It can be different every time you make it. You can make it with whatever fruit you find growing around your house or stored in your refrigerator or canning shelves. Use your imagination—and what you find.

2.   Fruits have bold, bright colors. Think about that when you choose fruits to mix together. Make your salad beautiful!

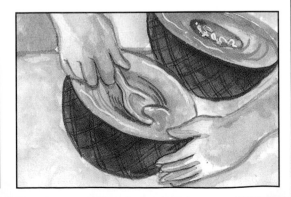

3. Fruits have different textures— soft, crunchy, and springy. Choose a variety of textures when you pick fruits to mix together. Make your salad fun to eat!

4. Many fruits have peels or rinds. We do not eat many of them, like the peels of a banana or the shell of a cantaloupe. But we do eat some peels —and they add bright color and texture. Think about that when you are deciding whether or not to remove the peel.

5. Most fruit should be washed before it is eaten. Do it thoroughly but gently so you don't damage it.

6. Ask your adult helper to work with you in cutting off peels and taking out seeds. Then when the fruit is ready for chopping or slicing, you can take over with the cutting board and paring knife.

Make the chunks big enough that people know what fruit they're eating. Make the chunks small enough that people can get several different kinds of fruit on the spoon at one time. Then they can enjoy the wonderful mix of flavors and textures in each bite.

7. If you like juicy fruit salad, be sure to use at least one jar of canned fruit. If you use all canned fruit, you will have more juice than you need, so *spoon* some of the fruit out of the jar or can, rather than pouring all the fruit and its juice into the mixing bowl.

8. Stir the mixture all together with great care so you don't smash the little pieces of fruit. Then, when it's well mixed, enjoy a bowlful, no matter what time it is. Or eat it with your main meal, or as dessert. Fruit salad brightens up everything.

Macaronis with Cheese— and Hamburger

Serves 4-6, 1-cup servings

Skill Level:

INGREDIENTS

- 1$\frac{1}{2}$ quarts water
- 2 tsp. salt
- 1 cup uncooked macaronis
- $\frac{1}{4}$ cup onion, chopped
- 1 green pepper, chopped
- $\frac{1}{2}$ pound hamburger
- 2 Tbsp. flour
- 1 cup canned tomatoes
- 1 cup grated cheese
- shortening
- 2 Tbsp. margarine
- $\frac{1}{2}$ cup bread crumbs or cracker crumbs

EQUIPMENT

- Three-quart saucepan
- Measuring cups
- Measuring spoons
- Wooden spoon
- Colander
- Cutting board
- Paring knife
- Grater
- Paper towel
- 1$\frac{1}{2}$-quart baking dish
- Small microwave-safe bowl

1. Put the water in the saucepan. Stir in the salt. Cover the pan and turn the stove on to medium.

2. When the water really boils, with big bubbles bouncing across the surface, slowly pour in the macaronis. Stir them well. Do not cover the pan.

3. Cook the macaronis for 10 minutes. Stir them every 3 or 4 minutes. Then turn off the stove.

4. Ask your grown-up helper to pour the macaronis into the colander to drain. (If you are tall enough to do this yourself, you may need hot pads to hold the pan. Be careful, too, not to steam your face.)

5. Put the hamburger in the saucepan that you've just used for the macaronis.

6. Then peel the onion and wash it. (See page 44 for an explanation about how to chop it.) Put the onion pieces in the saucepan on top of the hamburger.

7. Wash the green pepper. Ask for help to cut out the core. Lay the pepper on the cutting board and cut it in half. Pull out all the little seeds from inside.

8. Cut one pepper half lengthwise into narrow strips. Then pile up three or four strips and cut across them about every $1/4$-inch to make little cubes. Push the pieces off the cutting board into the pan with the hamburger and onion. Finish the first half of the green pepper this way.

Do the exact same thing with the second half of the pepper. Add it all to the saucepan.

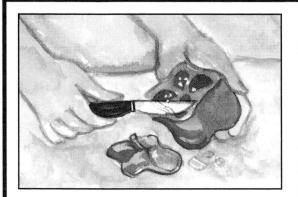

9. Set the pan on the stove and turn it to medium heat. Carefully break up the hamburger with the wooden spoon, and stir the onion, green pepper, and hamburger together.

Stir the mixture about every 3 minutes so it doesn't stick and burn and so that all the meat browns.

10. When the hamburger is browned all over, add the flour and tomatoes. Stir well and cook for 5 more minutes.

11. Set the pan on a hot pad on the counter. Spoon in the macaronis and mix it all together well.

12. Stand the grater on the cutting board. Hold the top of the grater firmly with one hand and rub the piece of cheese over the big holes of the grater with your other hand. Be watchful so that you don't catch your fingers on the grater's sharp edges.

13. Stir the grated cheese in with the meat and macaroni mixture.

14. Set the oven to 375°.

15. Grease the inside of the baking dish with shortening on a paper towel. Spoon the meat-vegetables-macaroni mix into the dish.

16. Cut the margarine into small chunks and put it in the small microwave-safe bowl. Microwave it on high for 1 minute.

17. Stir the bread crumbs and melted margarine together. Sprinkle that over the meat and macaronis.

18. Bake for 25 minutes.

Ham, Potatoes, and Green Beans

Serves 6-8, 1-cup servings

Skill Level:

INGREDIENTS

- 2-3 lb. ham shoulder or picnic, or 1-2 lb. ham hock
- $1/2$ cup water
- 4 potatoes
- 1 quart green beans

EQUIPMENT

- Roaster with lid (or heavy-duty tin foil to cover roaster)
- Measuring cup
- Vegetable peeler
- Paring knife
- Serving spoon

1. Set the oven to 350°.

2. Place the piece of ham in a roaster. Pour in $1/2$ cup water and cover the roaster tightly. Bake for 1-$1^1/2$ hours. (Use the longer time if you have a heavier piece of meat.)

3. While the ham is baking, wash the potatoes, and then carefully peel them. Cut them into chunks that are about two inches across.

4. When it is time to add the vegetables to the meat, set the roaster on the counter. Lay the potato chunks around the ham (being careful not to steam yourself or touch the pan). Then spoon the green beans around the ham, beside and on top of the potatoes.

5. Cover the roaster again and put it back in the oven. Bake for one more hour.

6. When the meal is finished baking, ask a grown-up to help you cut the meat into individual serving-sized chunks. Serve the meal straight from the roaster or from a large platter.

Beef Roast

INGREDIENTS

- Beef roast
  (If the meat has a bone in it, tell the shopper in your family you will need about $1/3$ pound for each person. If the meat has no bone, you will need about $1/4$ pound for each person who will be eating.)
- Salt
- Pepper
- Water

EQUIPMENT

- Roaster with a lid
- One or two meat forks

1. Put the piece of meat in the roaster. Using a salt shaker, sprinkle the top and sides of the meat lightly with salt. Shake a few dashes of pepper over it, too, from the pepper shaker.

2. Turn the meat over and do the same thing. Flip it back.

3. Turn the oven to 325°.

4. Add water to the pan —just enough so that when you put the tip of your finger against the inside bottom of the roaster, the water comes up to your first knuckle.

5. Cover the pan and put it in the oven. Ask an adult who is working with you to help you decide how long to roast the meat.

If the meat is a tender cut (a rib or a high quality rump roast), roast it about 25 minutes for each pound.

If it is a chuck or less tender rump roast, bake it about 50 minutes for each pound.

6. When the meat is finished roasting, lift it onto a serving platter with one or two big forks. Ask a grown-up to help you, depending upon how big the roast is.

You are ready to make the gravy, while your adult helper slices the meat.

Gravy

Serves 5, ½-cup servings

Skill Level: ◆ ◆

INGREDIENTS

- ½ cup cold water
- ¼ cup plus 1 Tbsp. flour
- 2 cups broth from the roaster

EQUIPMENT

- One-quart jar with lid
- Measuring cups
- Measuring spoons
- Microwave-safe medium-sized mixing bowl
- Dipper
- Whisk

1. While the meat is roasting, put the cold water in the jar. Add the flour to it. Put on the lid and shake the jar up and down and around and around until all the lumps of flour disappear. Then set it aside until you need it.

2. After you've taken the meat out of the roaster, dip the broth left in the roaster into a measuring cup. Measure 2 cups and pour the broth into the mixing bowl.

3. Microwave the broth on High for 1-1½ minutes, or until it is boiling. Set the bowl on a hot pad on the counter.

4. Shake the jar with the flour-water mixture again to be sure it is well mixed. Then slowly pour about half of it into the hot broth. Whisk the mixture together and watch it begin to thicken.

Add the rest of the flour and water; then whisk it all together again.

If it isn't as thick as you would like, microwave the broth on high for one minute. Take it from the microwave and whisk it. By now it should be like gravy, ready to be ladled over the sliced meat and mashed potatoes (page 54)!

53

Mashed Potatoes

Serves 6, ½-cup servings

Skill Level: ◆ ◆ ◆

INGREDIENTS

- 6 medium-sized potatoes
- ½-¾ cup milk
- ½ tsp. salt
- 4 Tbsp. butter

EQUIPMENT

- Vegetable peeler
- Paring knife
- Cutting board
- Two-quart microwave-safe bowl
- Measuring cups
- Small microwave-safe dish
- Measuring spoons
- Electric mixer with bowl or potato masher
- Small saucepan

1. Peel each potato with the vegetable peeler. With the end of the peeler, remove any potato eyes. (Eyes are the round, brown knots that stick out from the potato.) Be careful, because the blade on the vegetable peeler is sharp.

2. Next, with a sharp knife, cut the potatoes into pieces about an inch wide and long.

3. Put the potato pieces into a 2-quart microwave-safe cooking pot and cover them with water.

4. Cook the potatoes until they are very soft. Microwave on high for about 16 minutes, stirring every 4 minutes.

5. While the potatoes are cooking, pour ½ cup of milk into a small microwave-safe dish. When the potatoes are finished cooking, heat the milk until a "skin" forms on its surface. That will take about 1½ minutes on High in the microwave.

6. When the potatoes are soft, pour them, the milk, and the salt into a mixer bowl. Using an electric mixer on medium speed, mash the potatoes until they are smooth, without any lumps.

You may use a potato masher instead of an electric mixer. Stomp the potatoes, milk, and salt together in the mixer bowl until all the lumps are gone. Be careful not to splash yourself!

7. Pour mashed potatoes into a serving bowl. Add brown butter.

BROWN BUTTER

1. Put about 4 Tbsp. butter into a small saucepan.

2. Set the saucepan on the stove and turn it to a medium heat.

3. Watch the butter until it begins to turn brown. After it becomes a medium brown, turn off the burner and pour the butter over the mashed potatoes or vegetables. Watch that the butter does not burn when you are browning it.

Sweet Pickles

Skill Level:

INGREDIENTS

- 1 quart medium-sized cucumbers cut in 1-inch chunks
- 2 Tbsp. salt
- Boiling water
- $3/4$ cup sugar
- $3/4$ cup apple cider vinegar
- $1/4$ cup water
- $1/8$ tsp. turmeric
- $1/4$ tsp. dry mustard
- $1/4$ tsp. allspice
- $1/4$ tsp. mustard seed
- $1/4$ tsp. celery seed

EQUIPMENT

- Cutting board
- Paring knife
- Large mixing bowl
- Microwave-safe medium-sized mixing bowl
- Colander
- Two- or three-quart saucepan
- Measuring cups
- Measuring spoons
- Wooden spoon
- 8-oz. jelly jars with lids

1. Scrub the cucumbers well. Lay them, one at a time, on the cutting board and cut off both ends. Then slice each cucumber into 1-inch chunks. (That's about as long as the spoon part of a one-tsp. measuring spoon.

2. Put the pieces in a large mixing bowl. Cover with 2 Tbsp. salt and set the cucumbers aside.

3. Fill the microwave-safe bowl about half-full of water. Microwave it on High for 5 minutes, or until it boils.

4. If the microwave-safe bowl has a spout, pour the boiling water over the cucumber chunks until they are covered. If the bowl doesn't have a spout, ask a grown-up to help you pour the water.

5. Let the water and the cucumbers stand overnight.

6. When you have time the next day, spoon the cucumber pieces into a colander and pour the water away. Let the cucumbers continue to drain.

7. Measure the sugar, vinegar, $1/4$ cup water, and spices into the saucepan. Stir them together until the sugar disappears.

8. Turn on the stove to a medium heat and let the mixture heat until it begins to boil. Watch for little bubbles to roll the whole way across the top of the liquid. When that happens, turn

off the stove and lift the pan onto a hot pad on the counter.

9. Spoon the cucumber chunks into the sweet-sour mixture, being careful not to splash yourself with the hot syrup.

10. Put the pan back on the stove and turn the heat to medium. Cook it until the mixture begins to boil again. Then turn off the stove.

11. The cucumbers have become pickles! Fill up the little jelly jars with pickles and juice. Cover them when they're cool. Refrigerate your own and give the rest away to friends.

Chocolate Cake

INGREDIENTS

- $1^1/_2$ cups sugar
- $^1/_2$ cup vegetable oil
- 2 eggs
- $^1/_2$ cup buttermilk or sour milk
- 3 heaping Tbsp. cocoa powder
- 1 cup boiling water
- $2^1/_2$ cups flour
- 2 tsp. baking powder
- 1 tsp. baking soda
- $^1/_4$ tsp. salt
- 1 tsp. vanilla

EQUIPMENT

- Measuring cups
- Measuring spoons
- Large mixer bowl
- Electric mixer or sturdy wooden spoon
- Small bowl
- Medium-sized bowl
- Wooden spoon
- Plastic spatula
- 9" x 13" cake pan
- Dipper

1. Put the sugar and oil into the mixer bowl and beat on medium speed with the mixer—or stir with the wooden spoon—until the batter becomes a light yellow color.

2. Turn off the mixer. Break the eggs into a small bowl, then slide them into the mixer bowl. Add the buttermilk or sour milk, too. (Here's how you make sour milk—put 2 tsp. lemon juice or vinegar in a $^1/_2$-cup measure. Fill the cup with milk and let it sit for a few minutes.)

3. Beat on medium speed or by hand until the batter is smooth. Turn off the mixer.

4. Place the cocoa powder in a medium-sized bowl. Pour the boiling water in slowly. Stir until the mixture begins to thicken.

5. Pour the hot cocoa into the batter and mix on medium speed, or by hand, until it is well blended. Turn off the mixer and scrape the sides of the bowl with a spatula.

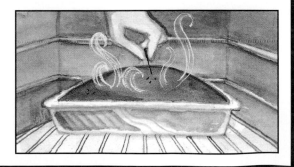

6. To the batter add all the dry ingredients—the flour, baking powder, baking soda, and salt—plus, the vanilla. Mix together on medium speed, or by hand, until there are no lumps and the mixture is smooth. Turn off the mixer and scrape the bowl and beaters.

7. Turn the oven to 350°.

8. Grease a long 9" x 13" cake pan with shortening. Spoon 3 Tbsp. flour into the greased pan and shake it until the bottom is lightly covered. Then, holding the pan over the sink, turn the pan up so the flour falls onto the one side. Keep turning the pan and bumping it gently with one hand so the flour falls onto the other sides. Dump the excess flour into the sink.

9. Dip the batter into the greased and floured pan. Bake for 20-25 minutes. After 20 minutes, check if the cake is done by sticking a toothpick into the center of the cake. If it comes out clean, the cake is finished and you may take it out of the oven. Place it on a wire rack to cool.

If batter sticks to the toothpick, bake the cake for another one or two minutes. Check again. Repeat until the toothpick comes out clean.

Caramel Frosting

Frosting for one 9" x 13" cake

Skill Level: ◆ ◆

INGREDIENTS

- $\frac{1}{2}$ cup butter or margarine
- 1 cup brown sugar
- $\frac{1}{4}$ cup milk
- $1\frac{3}{4}$-2 cups confectioners' sugar

EQUIPMENT

- Medium-sized microwave safe bowl
- Table knife
- Measuring cups
- Wooden spoon
- Flour sifter
- Waxed paper

3.　Stir in the milk. Microwave on High for 30 seconds. Stir until the mixture is well blended. Microwave on High for another 30 seconds. Stir again. Continue doing this until the mixture boils.

4.　Then set the bowl on the counter to cool. While you are waiting, sift the confectioners' sugar onto a big sheet of waxed paper.

1.　Put the butter or margarine in the microwave-safe bowl. Place it in the microwave. Set it on High for $1\frac{1}{2}$ minutes. Microwave it another 20 seconds if the butter is not fully melted.

2.　Stir in the brown sugar until it is well mixed. Microwave on Power 8 for one minute.

5. When the butter-sugar-milk mixture reaches room temperature, measure one cup of the sifted confectioners' sugar and dump it into the cooked mixture. Stir it gently (so you don't have clouds of sugar in your face!) until there are no lumps.

6. If the frosting is runny, add another $1/4$ cup of confectioners' sugar. Stir until it is smooth. If you can now spread the frosting with a table knife, do not add more confectioners' sugar.

7. If the frosting is still runny, add another $1/4$ cup of confectioners' sugar and stir it in. Continue adding this sugar until you can spread the frosting. When you reach that point, spread it on your cooled cake right away, before the frosting hardens.

Baked Corn

Serves 6-7, ½-cup servings

Skill Level: ◆ ◆

INGREDIENTS

- 2 eggs
- 2 Tbsp. butter
- 2 cups corn, creamed or whole kernels
- 1 cup milk
- 1½ rounded Tbsp. cornstarch
- 2 Tbsp. sugar
- ½ tsp. salt
- Dash of pepper
- Shortening

EQUIPMENT

- Microwave-safe little mixing bowl
- Blender, or a large mixing bowl with a wooden spoon, instead
- Measuring cups
- Table knife
- Measuring spoons
- Plastic spatula
- Paper towel
- 1-1½-quart baking dish

2. Put 2 Tbsp. butter in the small mixing bowl and microwave it on High for 45 seconds. Add it to the blender.

3. Put in all the rest of the ingredients except the shortening.

1. Crack the eggs into a small bowl. If you are using a blender, slide the eggs into It, cover the blender, and turn it on until the egg whites and yolks are just blended. (If you are not using a blender, do steps 1-4 in a large mixing bowl with a wooden spoon.)

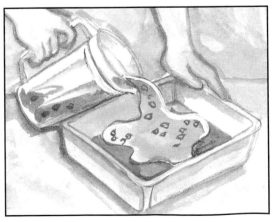

4. Blend the mixture for 10 seconds. Stop and stir the mixture up from the bottom. Blend another 10 seconds.

5. Grease the inside of the baking dish with a dab of shortening on a paper towel.

6. Set the oven at 350°.

7. Pour the blended corn into the casserole dish, cleaning out the blender (or mixing bowl) with a plastic spatula.

8. Set the oven to 350°.

9. Bake the corn for 1 hour or a little longer, until it is firm and custardy.

Creamed Dried Beef

Serves 6, ½-cup servings

Skill Level:  ◆ ◆

INGREDIENTS

- 4 Tbsp. margarine
- ¼ pound thinly sliced dried beef
- 4 Tbsp. flour
- 2½ cups milk
- 3 or 4 medium-sized potatoes

EQUIPMENT

- Measuring spoons
- Table knife
- Microwave-safe medium-sized mixing bowl
- Wooden spoon
- Whisk
- Measuring cups
- Fork
- Paper towel

1. Cut the margarine into chunks and drop them into the microwave-safe mixing bowl. Microwave the margarine on High for 1 minute. If it is not completely melted, microwave it on High for 20 more seconds.

2. Remove the bowl from the microwave. Tear the dried beef slices into shreds and drop them into the melted margarine. Stir together well to coat all the dried beef pieces with margarine.

3. Put the bowl with the dried beef back in the microwave for 2 minutes on High. Take it out and stir it. Put it back in for another 2 minutes on High. Take it out and stir it. Put it back in for another 2 minutes on High. By now the edges of the dried beef should be getting brown and crispy.

4. Stir in the flour until it sticks to all the pieces of dried beef. Microwave on High for 2 minutes.

5. Carefully pour the milk into the bowl with the dried beef. Stir together gently with the wooden spoon.

6. Microwave the mixture on High for 2½ minutes. Take it out and stir it with a whisk.

7. Microwave it again on High for 2½ minutes. Take it out and stir it again with a whisk. The mixture should be starting to get thick, like gravy.

8. Microwave on High for 1½ minutes. Stir with a whisk. Microwave again on High for 1½ minutes and stir. Repeat these steps until the mixture boils and is quite thick. When that happens, cover it with plastic and set it aside until the potatoes are ready.

9. Wash and dry the potatoes. Jag each one 2 or 3 times with a fork.

10. Lay the paper towel in the microwave and put the potatoes in, one on each corner of the towel. Microwave on High for 3 minutes.

11. Turn each potato over and microwave on High for 3 more minutes. Let the potatoes rest for 2 minutes.

12. Jag the potatoes with a fork. If they are tender, split them open and cover them with the creamed dried beef.
    If they are still somewhat hard, microwave them on High for another 2 minutes before you eat them.

Candied Sweet Potatoes

Serves 6

Skill Level:

INGREDIENTS

- 6 medium-sized sweet potatoes
- $^1/_4$ cup butter or margarine
- $^1/_4$-$^1/_2$ cup brown sugar

EQUIPMENT

- Vegetable brush
- Paper towel
- Fork
- Paring knife
- Cutting board
- Skillet or frying pan
- Measuring cups
- Wooden spoon
- Metal spatula

1. Wash the sweet potatoes well. You may use a vegetable brush to get the dirt out of all the nooks and crannies if you scrub lightly (watch that you don't damage the potatoes). Dry the potatoes.

2. Lay a paper towel in the microwave. Put 3 of the potatoes on the towel, heavier ends away from the center of the oven, so that the potatoes lie like spokes of a wheel. Try to space them evenly in the oven so the heat reaches each one equally.

3. Microwave on High for 3 minutes. Turn each potato over (use a pot holder or a fork). Microwave for another minute on High. Jag each potato's thick end with a fork to see if it is tender—when the fork slides right in. If it is, place the potato on a plate to cool. If it is still hard, microwave on High for one more minute. Jag again to see if it is tender.

When these 3 potatoes are tender, place the remaining 3 potatoes in the oven and repeat the process.

4. Let all the potatoes cool until you can handle them without burning your fingers.

Then peel them, either by gently rubbing the skins off with your fingers, or by using a paring knife. Lift up an edge of the skin and slowly pull it up. The skin should come off in long strips.

5. Throw away the skins. Put the peeled potatoes in the refrigerator for 30 minutes or more. Cooled potatoes slice more easily.

6. When you are ready to cut them, lay one potato at a time on the cutting board and slice it lengthwise into $1/4$- to $1/2$-inch slices. Lay the slices on a plate until you've prepared the syrup.

7. Melt the butter or margarine in a skillet. Add the brown sugar and, with a wooden spoon, stir it in until it melts.

8. Turn the heat lower so you don't burn yourself with this next step. Lay as many sweet potato slices as you can into the syrup, making sure each slice lies flat against the bottom of the pan.

Turn the heat to simmer and cook the potatoes until they begin to brown. Use a metal spatula to lift them up to check whether they are brown enough to turn over.

When they are dark brown, turn them gently so you don't splash yourself. Brown them on the topside; then remove them to a platter.

Add any slices that didn't fit in the skillet the first time and brown them, too, on both sides.

Chicken Pot Pie

Serves 8, 1-cup servings

Skill Level: ◆ ◆ ◆

INGREDIENTS

- 2 13³/₄-oz. cans chicken broth
- 3 5-oz. cans chicken, cooked and cut up
- 2 medium-sized potatoes
- 1 small onion
- Salt and pepper
- 8-ozs. pot pie noodles

EQUIPMENT

- Large cooking pot
- Vegetable peeler
- Paring knife
- Cutting board
- Serving spoon
- Wooden spoon

1. Pour the chicken broth into a large cooking pot. Turn the stove on to medium high.

2. As you wait for the broth to simmer (simmering is when little bubbles begin to appear around the outside edge of the hot broth), peel the four potatoes with a vegetable peeler. Make sure you get all the peels off. Cut out the eyes (the brown knotty things that stick out of the potato) with the end of your vegetable peeler. Remember, vegetable peelers are sharp and the blades can cut you.

3. Carefully, with a sharp knife and the cutting board, cut the potatoes into chunks about one-inch square.

4. With the same knife, chop the onions into very small pieces (see page 44 for directions).

5. When the broth begins to simmer, lower the potatoes and onions into the broth with a big spoon so you don't splash yourself. Cook them until they become soft.

7. Cut open the bag of pot pie noodles and slowly add them to the broth (if you drop them in too quickly the broth might splash you.) Add the chicken and cook everything for about 20 minutes. Stir every 5 minutes with a wooden spoon.

8. Turn off the burner and ladle the chicken pot pie into bowls or a serving dish.

6. Keep on cooking until the broth begins to boil. Boiling is when large bubbles appear in the broth. This happens after it has been simmering for a while.

SPECIAL TIMES

Special times are celebrated with special food. And usually lots of it!

THE SCHOOL PICNIC

At the end-of-school picnic, parents bring baskets full of food. One father drives a clean-swept farm wagon into the schoolyard. Mothers cover it with clean tablecloths, then bring out a spread of casseroles, cakes and candies, salads, puddings, and all kinds of amazing favorites—for everybody to share.

IN THE FIELDS

Hot, sweaty days with the horses in the fields go better with a snack of homemade sugar cookies and lemonade.

You can brighten up hay-cutting or corn-cultivating or the barley harvest with cold homemade root beer and oatmeal cookies with raisins.

The boys and girls who aren't old enough to help in the fields, but are big enough to help bake, load up their express wagon with the treats. Then they make a mid-afternoon visit to the fields. The outdoor work crew gets a break, but doesn't have to come the whole way to the house. The kitchen crew gets a lot of satisfaction watching the cookies and drink disappear!

FAMILY REUNIONS

Big families plan reunions so they are sure to see all their aunts and uncles and cousins and nieces and nephews. The children play ball and house and horse. The grown-ups talk and visit. And everybody eats.

Everybody brings food to share—often the dishes they're famous for. That means there is a lot of variety, and that one family doesn't need to do all the work.

SUNDAY LUNCH

The Amish meet for church services in their homes. They don't have church buildings. Every family gets a turn to host Sunday morning church about twice a year.

After church, the family serves everyone lunch. Each Sunday it's the same menu. That is kind to the cooks, who don't have to think about making something outstanding or worry that they've made food that people won't like.

It's the kind of meal you can make ahead of time, since it would be hard to cook when there are people sitting everywhere in your house (including the kitchen). Besides, you don't want to be stirring and making a racket in the kitchen when someone is speaking or praying or singing. And you must be able to serve it fast because everyone is hungry when the $3^1/_2$-4 hour church service is over.

THE MENU

* Homemade Bread with Butter and
    Jelly
* Peanut Butter and Molasses Spread
* Cheese Cubes or Schmierkase (sort
    of like homemade cottage cheese)
* Pickles
    Pickled Red Beets
* Schnitz Pie
    Coffee and Tea

* recipes are in this book

WEDDING FOOD

Weddings are really big celebrations. They are usually held at the bride's home. (Remember the Amish have no church buildings.) Home is where all the important times in a person's life happens—Amish children are almost always born at home, they work at home, they have church at home, plus their parties and family get-togethers. So getting married at home makes sense. And Amish houses are built especially for hosting big groups.

The family pushes back the first floor walls of the house. The walls slide into big pockets or can be folded up and carried away. Then the family sets up rows of benches for the guests. After a long wedding ceremony, helpers set up long tables all through the first floor, and the people start to eat. And eat. And eat some more.

When the afternoon games and singing are over, the cooks bring out more food!

All day, special homemade cakes and candies and salads and finger-food trays sit on tables in the first floor rooms and even in the basement! It is a feast day.

A WEDDING DINNER MENU

  Chicken Roast
* Mashed Potatoes and * Gravy
  Cole Slaw
  Creamed Celery
* Applesauce
* Bread and Butter
  Canned Peaches
  Canned Pears
  Spiced Cantaloupe
  Doughnuts
  Custard Pies
  Fruit Pies
  Layer Cakes
* Sugar Cookies
  Potato Chips
  Coffee

* recipes are in this book

TREATS AND SNACKS

Children need snacks because they are growing and active. For example, walking to and from school takes a lot of energy. Grown-ups who work hard in the garden and yard and house and barn and fields get hungry between meals, too, and sometimes before bedtime.

Some snacks help keep you happy until the next meal. Other snacks cool you off if you've been pulling sweet corn or canning peaches or gathering eggs. There are snacks to relax with—when Datt has finished in the barn and Mamm has all the sewing put away and evening is coming. Then all the family takes their drinks and munchies to the yard swing or the porch and watches the sun go down and the lightning bugs come out.

A SNACK FOR SNOW DAYS

* Snow Ice Cream

A SNACK FOR A LONG AFTERNOON OR EVENING

* Soft Pretzels

* recipes are in this book

Peanut Butter and Molasses Spread

Skill Level: ◆

INGREDIENTS

- ¹/₄ cup smooth peanut butter
- ¹/₄ cup molasses

EQUIPMENT

- Small mixing bowl
- Measuring cups
- Table knife
- Plastic spatula
- Wooden spoon

1. With a table knife, scoop peanut butter from its container into the ¹/₄ cup. Empty the cup into the mixing bowl.

2. Pour the molasses into the same measuring cup, and then empty it into the bowl holding the peanut butter. (Be sure to clean out the cup with a plastic spatula.)

3. Mix the peanut butter and molasses together well until creamy.

4. Spread on bread or crackers. (To make it easier to spread, warm the mixture in the microwave on High for 10 seconds.)

Schnitz Pie

Makes 1 9" pie

Skill Level: ◆ ◆ ◆ ◆

FILLING INGREDIENTS

- 3 cups dried apples
- $2\frac{1}{4}$ cups warm water
- 1 tsp. lemon extract
- $\frac{2}{3}$ cup brown sugar
- 1 9" unbaked pie shell, plus a top crust

PIE CRUST INGREDIENTS

- $1\frac{1}{4}$ cups flour
- $\frac{1}{4}$ tsp. salt
- $\frac{1}{2}$ cup vegetable shortening
- 1 small egg
- 2 Tbsp. cold water
- 1 tsp. vinegar
- Flour

EQUIPMENT FOR FILLING

- Measuring cups
- Medium-sized saucepan
- Wooden spoon
- Measuring spoons
- Potato masher
- Dipper or big spoon

FOR PIE CRUST

- Large mixing bowl
- Measuring cups
- Measuring spoons
- Wooden spoon
- Table knife
- Plastic spatula
- Pastry cutter
- Small mixing bowl
- Fork
- Rolling pin
- Pastry cloth
- Pie plate

Dried sliced apples, or schnitz (from the German word for "cut"), are sometimes sold in health food stores or other special food stores.

1. Measure the apple slices into the saucepan. Pour the warm water over top of them. With a wooden spoon push the slices down into the water so they're well covered. Let them sit for about 30 minutes.

2. Move the saucepan with the apples and water to the stove and cook them over medium heat until they get mushy. Stir them every 3 or 4 minutes so they don't stick to the bottom of the pan.

3. When they are real soft, take them off the stove and add the lemon and sugar. Mash them together with the potato masher until they are well mixed.

4. Set the oven to 425°.

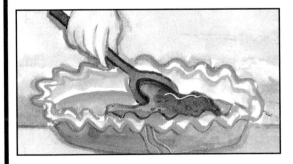

5. Ladle the mixture into the unbaked pie shell. Cover it with a crust and pinch the top and bottom edges together. Cut 5 or 6 slashes (each an inch long) in the top crust to keep the filling from cooking out. Make a design with the slashes!

6. Bake the pie at 425° for 15 minutes. Then turn the oven back to 350° and bake the pie for another 30 minutes. Lift it out of the oven and onto a rack to cool.

PIE CRUST

Ask a grown-up to be nearby when you do this the first few times.

1. Measure the flour and salt into the mixing bowl and stir them together.

2. Scoop the shortening into the measuring cup with a table knife. Put it into the bowl with the dry ingredients, using a plastic spatula to clean out the measuring cup.

3. Using the pastry cutter—or your fingers—work the shortening into the flour thoroughly until it forms little peas or crumbs. Set this aside until you need it.

4. In a small mixing bowl beat the egg. Add the cold water and vinegar, stirring them all together.

5. Pour this mixture into the crumbs and, with a sturdy table fork, mix it all together. Soon a ball will form. Chase it around the bowl, gathering up all the loose crumbs that you can. Then set the bowl with the pie dough in the refrigerator for 20 to 30 minutes.

6. Meanwhile, spread the pastry cloth on a big flat surface. Sprinkle flour over it. Move your pie plate nearby.

7. When the dough is cooled, flour your hands and sprinkle flour on the rolling pin. Cut off about $^2/_3$ of the ball of dough and lay it in the center of the pastry cloth. (You'll need the other chunk of dough later.)

8. Flatten the dough with the heel of your hand, then roll it out into a big circle, about 12 inches across. Always roll from the center out to the edges to keep the dough from getting thin in spots.

9. When you've finished rolling the dough, fold the top part of the circle down until the top edge reaches the bottom edge. But don't press down; you don't want the circle to stick together. Then fold the left edge over to meet the right edge (again, don't press together!).

10. Carefully lift the dough up and lay it in one-quarter of the pie plate. Unfold the dough and settle it into the pie plate and up along the sides. If the

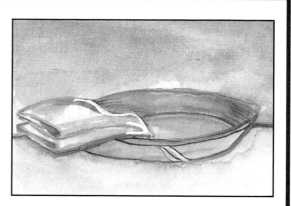

dough reaches out over the edge, fold it under so the top of the dough is even with the top of the pie plate.

11. When you have filled the crust with the schnitz mixture, dust the pastry cloth with flour and roll out the remaining dough. Fold it into quarters and lay it on top of the filling.

12. Pinch the top and bottom crusts together between your thumb and first finger, the whole way around the top to create a ripple effect.

Sugar Cookies

Makes 2½ dozen cookies

Skill Level: ◆ ◆ ◆

INGREDIENTS

- ³/₄ cup sugar
- ¹/₂ cup margarine or shortening
- 1 egg
- ¹/₂ cup buttermilk or sour cream
- 1¹/₂ cups plus 3 Tbsp. flour
- 1 tsp. baking powder
- ¹/₂ tsp. baking soda
- ¹/₂ tsp. vanilla
- Raisins (one for each cookie)
- Sugar (to sprinkle on top of each cookie)

EQUIPMENT

- Measuring cups
- Measuring spoons
- Large mixer bowl
- Electric mixer or wooden spoon
- Plastic spatula
- Small bowl
- Cookie sheets
- Wire racks
- Metal spatula

1.   Let the margarine reach room temperature so it's easier to work with. Then cut it up in chunks and place it in the mixer bowl, along with ³/₄ cup of sugar. Cream them together with the mixer on medium speed or stir them together vigorously with a wooden spoon.

2.   Turn off the mixer and scrape the sides of the bowl with the plastic spatula. Break the egg into a small bowl; then slide it into the mixer bowl. Beat again on medium speed, or with the wooden spoon, until the batter is smooth.

3.   Turn off the mixer, scrape the bowl, and add the buttermilk or sour cream, the flour, baking powder, baking soda, and vanilla. Start the mixer up again to medium speed, or stir the additions in until the batter is creamy and smooth.

4.   Turn off the mixer and scrape the sides of the bowl and the beaters. Set the oven to 375°.

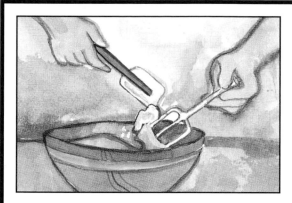

6. Put a raisin in the center of each cookie, pushing down gently so it doesn't fall off. Sprinkle lightly with sugar.

7. Bake for 8-10 minutes, until the cookies become a light brown.

8. Let them cool on a wire rack for several minutes before taking them off the cookie sheets with a metal spatula.

5. Grease two cookie sheets lightly. Drop the batter by teaspoonful onto the cookie sheets, keeping the cookies about two inches apart and about two inches away from the sides of the sheet.

Homemade Root Beer

Serves 16, 1-cup servings

Skill Level:

INGREDIENTS

- $1/2$ cup warm water
- 1 tsp. granulated yeast
- 1 quart hot water
- 2 cups sugar
- 4 tsp. root beer extract
- More warm water

EQUIPMENT

- Measuring spoons
- Small mixing bowl
- Large mixing bowl
- Long-handled wooden spoon
- Gallon jar

This recipe takes patience! Start at least one day before you want to drink the root beer. (Two days is better!) The root beer needs time to "work" and get fizzy.

1. Run water from the sink over the inside of your wrist until it feels quite warm. Fill $1/2$ cup with the warm water and pour it into a small mixing bowl. (You may use a microwave temperature probe to heat the water to 115°.)

2. Immediately add the yeast to the water (if the water cools too much, it won't make the yeast active), and stir gently until the yeast dissolves.

3. Pour 1 quart hot water into a large mixing bowl. Stir in the sugar until it dissolves.

4. Pour the yeast mixture, the sugar water, and the root beer extract into the gallon jar. Stir until all ingredients are well combined.

5. Fill the jar with warm water. Cover it. Set it in the warm sun for four hours. Then let it sit at room temperature for at least 24 hours (another day will make it peppier!).

6. Chill it in the refrigerator, or with ice cubes in individual glasses, before you drink it.

Snow Ice Cream

Serves 8-10, 1-cup servings

Skill Level: ◆

INGREDIENTS

- 2$\frac{1}{2}$ quarts clean snow
- $\frac{1}{2}$ cup milk
- 1 tsp. vanilla
- 1 cup sugar

EQUIPMENT

- Large mixing bowl
- Big long-handled spoon
- One-quart saucepan
- Measuring cups
- Measuring spoons

1. When there are several inches of fresh snow on the ground, scoop up just the top layer and pile it into the saucepan. (Don't dig too deep or you may pick up dirt. Don't wait too long after the snow stops falling or it may begin to gather dirt and dust from the air.)

2. When you've filled the saucepan once, dump it into the mixing bowl. Add one more full pan and then a half-full pan.

3. Gently mix in the milk, vanilla, and sugar until it has all disappeared.

4. Eat the ice cream right away!

Soft Pretzels

Makes 12 pretzels

Skill Level:

INGREDIENTS

- 1$\frac{1}{2}$ cups warm water
- 2 packages granulated yeast
- $\frac{1}{2}$ tsp. salt
- 4$\frac{1}{2}$ cups flour
- $\frac{1}{4}$ cup baking soda
- 1 cup cool water
- Shortening
- Salt (table or coarse)

EQUIPMENT

- Large microwave-safe mixing bowl
- Measuring cups
- Wooden spoon
- Measuring spoons
- Medium-sized mixing bowl
- Two cookie sheets
- Paper towel

This is a recipe that's even more fun to make with a bunch of friends!

1. Measure 1$\frac{1}{2}$ cups of water into the large mixing bowl. Use warm water from the faucet. Run the water over your wrist. When it feels quite warm, it is warm enough to make the yeast work. If you prefer, use the microwave temperature probe. When the water reaches 110°-115°, it will make the yeast work.

2. Stir in the two packs of yeast until it disappears.

3. Stir in the salt and up to 3$\frac{1}{2}$ cups of flour if you can. Ask your adult helper to stir if it gets too stiff for you.

4. Dump about $\frac{1}{2}$ cup of the flour that is left onto the counter. Spread it around where you will knead the dough, and dust some over your hands, too.

5. Roll the dough out of the bowl onto the flour and start to knead (See page 20 for instructions about kneading). When the dough gets sticky, add up to $\frac{1}{2}$ cup more flour.

6. When the dough is smooth and elastic and no longer sticky, put it back in the mixing bowl. Cover it with a tea towel and set it in the oven. Turn the oven light on, but not the oven itself. (The light makes the oven just a little bit warm.) Let the dough rest for 15 minutes.

7. Get out the dough and tear it into 12 equal pieces. Roll each piece into a rope shape, about 8 to 10 inches long.

8. Put 1 cup cool water in a medium-sized mixing bowl. Stir the baking soda into the water until it is dissolved. Then, one by one, soak each rope in the water-soda mixture for 2 minutes each.

9. Fish them out and shape each one into whatever shape you like—a pretzel, letters to spell your name or your friends', funny designs.

10. Grease each cookie sheet with shortening on a paper towel.

11. Set the oven to 350°.

12. Lift each shaped pretzel onto the greased cookie sheet (don't let the pretzels touch each other) and sprinkle them with either coarse or table salt.

13. Bake them for 20 minutes.

14. Eat the pretzels while they're warm! Share them with your friends.

Glossary

Boiling—The point at which liquid becomes so hot that it bubbles vigorously.

Broth—The liquid in which vegetables or meat have been cooked.

Colander—A bowl with lots of holes on the bottom and sides. Used for draining liquid from pasta and vegetables.

Cutting board—A small wooden or plastic board used for cutting up food.

Flour sifter—A container that, by turning or squeezing its handle, tosses flour lightly and then lets it fall through the wire netting on its bottom.

Grater—A flat sheet or 4-sided tool that is covered with different-sized holes. Each hole has a sharp edge so that it can slice or grate or chop food that is rubbed against it.

Kneading—Using your hands to push and pull dough on a flat surface to make it smooth and stretchy (see page 20).

Measuring cups—Cups of different sizes that measure one cup or parts of a cup. A set usually stacks one cup inside another and includes a $1/4$-cup size, a $1/3$-cup size, a $1/2$-cup size, and a one-cup size.

Measuring spoons—A nest of spoons that usually incudes a $1/4$-teaspoon size, a $1/2$-teaspoon size, a 1-teaspoon size, and a 1-tablespoon size.

Meat fork—A sturdy fork with long tines and a long handle, usually used for handling large cuts or slices of meat.

Metal spatula—A narrow metal blade with a handle used for lifting cooked eggs from a pan or cookies and pieces of cake from a baking pan.

Microwave-safe bowls—Cookware, usually made of plastic, glass, or ceramic, that can be safely used in a microwave. Bowls that contain metal are not safe to use in a microwave.

Mixing spoon—A sturdy, long-handled (if possible) spoon, made of metal or wood.

Plastic or rubber spatula—A narrow flexible blade, useful for cleaning batters and sauces from the inside of containers.

Paring knife—A knife with a sharp blade for cutting, chopping, slicing, and peeling.

Pastry cloth—A heavy piece of fabric, usually about one-yard square, on which pastry can be rolled out. The cloth allows the pastry to be folded and picked up easily.

Pastry cutter—A hand-held tool that has a handle on top with several thin but sturdy semi-circular wires attached to it. Used for making crumbs by cutting shortening into dry ingredients.

Schnitz—Dried apple slices.

Simmer—When a liquid is hot enough to have small bubbles breaking continually but gently across its surface.

Table knife—The kind of knife used as an eating utensil.

Vegetable peeler—A small metal gadget with a handle and a set of double blades, used to remove the skin of fruits and vegetables.

Whisk—A metal instrument with a handle and bulb-shaped top made of a series of sturdy looped wires, used for mixing.

Wire rack—A rack on which to set baked goods to cool. The open framework allows air to cool the bottom of the baked dish, as well as its sides and top.

Wooden spoon—A long-handled spoon, good for stirring since it doesn't scratch the bottom of a pan or bowl.

Index

About the Authors

Phyllis Pellman Good, Lancaster, Pennsylvania, has been involved in educating and writing about the Amish for more than 20 years. She is the author of numerous cookbooks, among them, *The Best of Amish Cooking*. Her most recent book is *A Mennonite Woman's Life*. She and her husband Merle are co-directors of The People's Place, in the village of Intercourse, Pennsylvania, an educational heritage center interpreting the Amish and Mennonites.

The Goods' daughters, Kate and Rebecca, have spent many days with Amish families during their preschool years and during summers through elementary and junior high school. These families provided love, fun, good food, and childcare for the two Good sisters on those days when their parents were both working away from home.

Mother and daughters have enjoyed their friendships with Amish families. They have discovered the pleasure of cooking together, and hope that this cookbook will offer many others the satisfaction of working together in the kitchen, as well as learning about the Amish community.